DESERT

ticktock

Copyright © **ticktock Entertainment Ltd 2006**
First published in Great Britain in 2006 by ticktock Media Ltd.,
Unit 2, Orchard Business Centre, North Farm Road, Tunbridge Wells, Kent TN2 3XF

ISBN 1 86007 856 7
Printed in China

Picture credits
t=top, b=bottom, c=centre, l=left, r=right
Ardea images: 17c. Alamy: 4-5, 9c. FLPA: 4-5, 6-7c, 10bl, 19c, 24br.
Every effort has been made to trace the copyright holders, and we apologise in advance for any unintentional omissions.
We would be pleased to insert the appropriate acknowledgements in any subsequent edition of this publication.

A CIP catalogue record for this book is available from the British Library.

contents

In the Desert

There is so much to see in the desert – from camels that carry men across this parched landscape to **deadly** creatures like snakes and scorpions.

What can you see in the desert?

Bighorn Sheep

Joshua Tree

Golden Eagle

Cactus

Rattlesnake

Bactrian Camel

Roadrunner

Gila Monster

Desert Tortoise

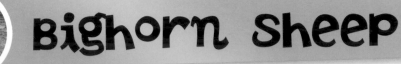

Bighorn Sheep can now be seen only in **remote** areas. All male sheep (rams) have big horns. The females (ewes) have smaller horns.

A ram's horns can measure 76 cm round the curl.

When these sheep have enough green plants to eat, they do not need to drink.

Bighorn rams fight a lot, usually to show who is stronger.

Bighorns rest during the day in summer, when it is very hot.

The Joshua Tree is found in only one part of the world – the Mojave Desert in Arizona, Nevada, Utah and South-west California.

The Joshua Tree can be anything from 4.5–12.2 metres tall.

Joshua Trees have **evergreen**, sword-shaped leaves and clusters of small, white flowers.

The tree was named after
Joshua in the Bible,
who pointed
the way to the
promised land.

 # GOLDen Eagle

The Golden Eagle is one of the largest birds of **prey** in the world. It gets its name from the golden feathers on its head.

Golden Eagles have broad wings, ideal for soaring high up in the mountains.

Golden Eagles use their razor-sharp beak to tear up food for their young chicks.

The eagle's powerful *talons*, hooked beak and keen eyesight all combine to make this bird a deadly **predator**.

cactus

There are many different types of cactus plant. They live happily in deserts because they can go without water for a long time.

Cacti can make a good home for birds.

Most cacti have **spines**. These help to protect the plant from being eaten by animals.

The inside of a cactus stem is spongy or **hollow**. This helps it to store water.

 # rattlesnake

This large, **venomous** snake is found only in North America. It is often caught by hunters, so it is becoming **rare**.

Horny **segments** that rattle when the tail is shaken give the snake its name.

Rattlesnakes, like all snakes, "smell" the air with their tongue.

The largest rattlesnake, the Eastern Diamondback, can be 2.4 metres long.

A Bactrian Camel has two humps. It uses them to store fat, which keeps it alive during a long journey in the desert.

Camels have hooved feet with thick pads that stop them sinking into the soft sand of the desert.

Bactrian Camels
live in central
Asia. In Arab
countries, camels
have one hump
and are called
Dromedaries.

Roadrunners are large birds with striped brown and white plumage.

Roadrunners live in deserts in western USA and Mexico.

The Roadrunner has **spindly** legs and a long tail that it carries high up in the air.

18

Spiky crest of feathers on head

Roadrunners can fly, but they prefer to walk or run. They can run fast enough to catch and eat rattlesnakes.

Gila Monster

The Gila Monster is a **poisonous** lizard with pink and black skin. It lives in the deserts of North America.

The Gila Monster has a long tongue and **fangs**.

Lizards are **cold-blooded** animals. They **bask** in the sun for warmth, and cool down in the shade.

The scaly skin of lizards helps to protect them from predators.

This tortoise spends most of its life under the soft sand of the desert. The sand protects it from the hot sun and the freezing cold nights.

The tortoise's soft body is covered by a hard shell called a carapace.

When the tortoise senses danger, it pulls its head, legs and tail back inside its shell.

22

The Desert Tortoise can live for up to 80 years. It eats grass, herbs and plants.

Glossary

Bask Lie in the sun to soak up its warmth

Cacti More than one cactus

Cold-blooded Animals with bodies that do not produce their own heat, and have to be heated or cooled by their surroundings

Deadly With the power to kill

Evergreen Staying green for the whole of the year

Fang A type of tooth that is sometimes hollow, so it can deliver poison as it bites

Hollow Being empty inside

Plumage The feathers on a bird

Predator An animal that hunts, kills and eats other animals

Prey An animal that is killed and eaten by another animal

Poisonous Containing a substance that can cause death or illness

Rare Something that is uncommon

Remote A place far away from towns and cities

Segments Parts that something can be divided into

Spine A sharp prickly point on a cactus or other plant

Spindly Long and thin

Talons Long, sharp claws used for holding and tearing apart prey

Venomous Containing venom (poison)